Employee

Handbook

A sample Employee Handbook Outline

Written by Kimball Hopson

(Business Operations Support Systems)

DISCLAIMER FOR BOOKS by Kimball Hopson

The books, videos, audio tapes, and other informational products offered by Kimball Hopson may offer a variety of clinical, business and health care related opinions, forms, procedures and must not replace the services of a licensed health care professional, lawyer or any current state or federal laws. This literature should not be used in the place of medical advice, diagnosis, business or treatment from your personal physician, lawyer, your state or federal regulations or health care professional. The products offered on Kimball Hopson present a broad range of information that may aid in making business startups for residential and Mental Health business. Each individual or business must adapt all forms and procedures to fit your state. These products were written for the State of California. **Kimball Hopson strongly recommends that you discuss any health concerns, or business decisions you may be considering, with your health care professionals or business consultants.**

(Business Operations Support Systems)

Your Company Name Here

"Your Company Motto here"

Employee

Handbook

Your Company Name Here

"Your Company Motto here"

Employment
Page 1

Benefits
Page11

Employee Handbook

Health & Safety
Page 16

Job Performance
Page 7

The following information is an overview of our company policies. Please see Your Company Name Here Management for questions or clarifications!

Time, Wage & Salary Administration
Page 4

Other Policies
Page 19

TABLE OF CONTENTS

TABLE OF CONTENTS
(continued)

TABLE OF CONTENTS
(continued)

Employment

Equal Employment Opportunity *(5/18/2015)*	There will be no discrimination by management, supervisors, or employees against an applicant or employee because of race, marital status, religion, color, national origin or ancestry, sex, age, disability, medical condition or veteran status. All matters relating to employment are based upon ability to perform the job, as well as dependability and reliability.
At-Will Employment *(5/18/2015)*	All employment and compensation with Your Company Name Here, is at-will. Employment can be terminated with or without cause, and with or without notice, at any time, at the option of either or Your Company Name Here, or yourself, except as otherwise provided by law. The at-will relationship between Your Company Name Here and its employees may not be changed or affected in any way except by a written agreement that states it is intended as a modification of a particular employee's at-will status, and is signed by the Administrator, on behalf of Your Company Name Here.
Newly Hired Employee Period *(5/18/2015)*	You are considered newly hired for the first four months of employment. Your first four months of employment is your initial opportunity to become acquainted with Your Company Name Here and your job responsibilities, and for Your Company Name Here to evaluate your performance. Completion of the newly hired period does not guarantee continued employment for any specified period of time, nor does it require that you be terminated only for "cause." Newly hired employees will receive holiday leave; all insurance required by law (disability, workers' compensation, unemployment, and social security) will be paid according to state and federal regulations. Medical, dental, and Section 125 benefits are not available during the first four months.
Employee Transfers *(5/18/2015)*	Your Company Name Here may initiate transfers as personnel requirements demand. You will be considered for job openings if you have been in your position for at least six months and have indicated an interest in transferring to another position. Transfers will be determined on the basis of merit, qualifications, and the needs of the company. If you wish to transfer from your position, you should first discuss the transfer with your immediate supervisor, and complete a Request to Transfer form. A list of approved job openings is available from the main office. If the position is filled with another candidate, you will retain your present position without prejudice or loss of benefits. If a transfer is initiated, the wage scale of the new position will apply.

Blank

Employee Relocation *(5/18/2015)*	All Your Company Name Here employees may be subject to relocation; if you are asked to relocate, and not able to accommodate this request, you may request a travel/hardship leave or be subject to termination.
Outside Employment *(5/18/2015)*	Your Company Name Here expects its full-time employees to consider their position with Your Company Name Here as primary employment. If you are a full-time employee, you must notify your supervisor prior to taking another job. Any outside employment must not create a conflict of interest, or interfere with your ability to properly perform job duties at Your Company Name Here. You will not be allowed to take an outside job with a competing company. If you are unable to maintain acceptable performance standards as a result of the outside employment, or if it is determined that a conflict of interest exists, permission to continue such employment may be rescinded, or you may be subject to disciplinary action, up to and including termination.
Lay-Off *(5/18/2015)*	On occasion, the needs of the company may require that certain employees be placed on lay-off status. Employees on lay-off status may be rehired. If you are laid off, your record will indicate an involuntary separation resulting from lay-off. The date of separation will be your last day worked. You may be considered for future openings prior to consideration of new applicants.
Resignation *(5/18/2015)*	An employee-initiated resignation is considered voluntary termination. If you resign, your resignation must be coordinated with your immediate supervisor and the Administrator. All company property must be returned to the company. If you have been absent for three consecutive days without notification, it may be assumed that you have voluntarily resigned. Your last day worked is the date of separation. Failure to return from an approved leave of absence may also be considered as resignation. The date of expiration of leave will be the separation date.

Resignation (cont.)	An exit interview is available for you upon your resignation. The company is interested in obtaining any information that will lead to the improvement of working conditions, management assistance and client assistance. The information you provide will be held in strict confidence and is only used to generate ideas for improvement. Employees who resign may purchase continued health and dental coverage by Your Company Name Here's medical insurance carrier under COBRA laws; you are responsible for payment of the full cost of this coverage.
Termination *(5/18/2015)*	Employment at Your Company Name Here is at will and may be terminated at any time, for any reason by you or by Your Company Name Here. All company property must be returned to the company. The "at will" relationship between Your Company Name Here and its employees may not be changed or affected in any way except by a written agreement that states it is intended as a modification of a particular employee's "at will" status, and is signed by the Administrator on behalf of Your Company Name Here. Employees terminated for gross misconduct are not entitled to COBRA benefits. Other terminated employees may purchase continued health and dental coverage by the company medical insurance carrier under COBRA laws, and are responsible for payment of the full cost of this coverage.
Net Credited Service *(5/18/2015)*	Your "Net Credited Service" is your total time of service with Your Company Name Here. If you are re-hired after a break in service at Your Company Name Here because you resigned or were terminated, previously earned net credited service can be bridged after three years of continuous service following your re-employment. For purposes of layoff, recall, promotion, job assignment and seniority-related benefits such as vacation, when you return from family leave, you will have no less seniority than when the leave began. Net credited service, however, does not accrue during any leave of absence in excess of 10 working days: your NCS date simply changes to reflect the time you were absent.

Time, Wage and Salary Administration

Hours of Work

(5/18/2015)

The normal workweek is 40 hours per week, Monday through Friday. Hours and days, however, may vary by facility or individual assignment according to the needs of the company.

Rest Periods:
Rest periods are with pay. Rest periods may not be used for making up time lost due to tardiness or absence. If you work fewer than 3 1/2 hours a day, you are not entitled to a rest period. If you work more than 3 1/2 hours, but fewer than 6 hours a day, you are entitled to one 15-minute rest period. If you work more than 6 hours a day, you are entitled to two 15-minute rest periods. If you work more than 10 hours a day, you are entitled to one additional 15-minute rest period.

Lunch Period:
If you are working more than 5 hours, you are required to take a minimum lunch period of one-half hour. When a work period of not more than 6 hours will complete the day's work, the meal period may be waived by the mutual consent of you and your supervisor. The standard lunch period is one hour; deviations from the standard must be approved by your supervisor, and may not result in overtime. Lunch periods are without pay.

Make-up Time:
Make-up time must be approved by your supervisor, must be applied in the same pay period, and cannot result in overtime. For example, if you wish to make up a 30-minute tardy from the morning, you may, with your supervisor's approval, take a 30-minute lunch period in order to work an additional 30 minutes as make-up time.

Attendance and Punctuality

(5/18/2015)

You are required to attend work regularly and be punctual, keeping absences to a minimum. If you need to be absent or late, you must notify your supervisor as soon as possible, but no later than 30 minutes of starting time; you must also tell your supervisor approximately how long you will be absent. If your immediate supervisor is unavailable, you should contact another facility supervisor or the Administrator. Except under emergency conditions, your friends, relatives or other employees may not notify your supervisor of absence or tardiness on your behalf.

With the exception of sick leave, you will not be paid for absences or tardiness. However, with the approval of your supervisor, time lost due to tardiness may be made up, provided that the make-up time does not result in overtime.

If you are absent due to an emergency situation, such as sudden illness or hospitalization, etc., your immediate supervisor should be notified within 24 hours. If your immediate supervisor is not available, the Administrator should be notified. A physician's statement may be required, at the company's discretion, for any absence due to illness or injury. Your Company Name Here may also request a corroborating statement from a company-appointed physician, at company expense.

Time Reporting *(5/18/2015)*	All employees are required by Your Company Name Here to prepare attendance reports. These reports are official company documents: falsifying/altering attendance reports, or punching/marking the time card of another employee are grounds for disciplinary action, up to and including termination.
Overtime *(5/18/2015)*	There may be times when you will need to work overtime so that we may successfully meet the needs of our customers. Your supervisor must approve all overtime in advance. If you repeatedly refuse to work overtime without satisfactory reason, you are not fulfilling the requirements of your position. This may be documented in your personnel file, and disciplinary action may be taken.
Time Off To Vote *(5/18/2015)*	You are encouraged to exercise your right to vote in primary, general and presidential elections, and are entitled to time off from work without loss of pay for this purpose. If you are a registered voter and do not have sufficient time outside of normal working hours to vote, you may request up to two hours time off, with pay, to vote at all general, direct primary, or presidential elections in accordance with applicable state laws. You must request time off to vote at least two working days before an election. Time off may be granted only at the beginning or end of the regular workday, and only when your regularly scheduled work hours do not leave sufficient time to vote outside of working hours. Time sheets must reflect the period of time off with pay for voting purposes and be approved by your immediate supervisor.
Payroll *(5/18/2015)*	*Paychecks are issued biweekly on Fridays for the period that has ended on the previous Sunday at 12:00 midnight.* When the payday is a holiday, you normally will be paid on Thursday. If you believe an error has been made on your paycheck, your supervisor should be notified immediately. By law, Your Company Name Here is required to deduct, where applicable, state and federal withholding taxes and garnishments from your pay. You are responsible for accurate completion of your W-4 form. Your contribution to the Medical Benefit and 401-K plans will also be deducted. All deductions will be itemized on the check stub. Each employee is responsible for providing the main office with current information regarding elective deductions, name, address, telephone number, and emergency contact. You must notify your supervisor of any changes in this information.

Wage and Salary Reviews *(5/18/2015)*	Wage and salary reviews are conducted annually. The company does not make automatic salary adjustments. In general, salary reviews will occur prior to September 1 of each year. Salary adjustment will be determined on a case-by-case basis, and is not automatic at these intervals.
Expense Reimbursement *(5/18/2015)*	Your Company Name Here will reimburse you for reasonable, pre-approved business expenses. You are responsible for keeping company expenses to a minimum. Records must be submitted for reimbursement on a monthly basis. You must keep accurate and complete records of all business expenses. All reimbursement requests must be submitted on the Expense Report Form by the 10th of each month for expenses incurred during the previous month. Your supervisor must approve your mileage and expense reports. Whenever possible, "trade" must be used for accommodations and meals. Allowable expenses for employees are air travel, car rental, hotel/motel, meals, mileage, other transportation, and parking/tolls.
Garnishment of Salary *(5/18/2015)*	The company will execute all garnishments and other wage attachment orders as required by law. Your Company Name Here expects you to manage your personal finances to avoid the necessity of a court-ordered wage assignment or garnishment. Repeated garnishments for more than one debt may result in your termination.

Job Performance

Standards of Conduct *(5/18/2015)*	A commitment to excellence is at the heart of the Your Company Name Here company policy. You represent the company while on the job, at company functions and whenever the public perceives you as representing the company. You are expected to maintain appropriate conduct at all times. The following examples of misconduct on your part are the types of conduct that will result in disciplinary action, including possible termination without prior warning. These are merely examples of misconduct, and are not intended to be a complete list. 1. Insubordination 2. Dishonesty 3. Intoxication/Influence of drugs 4. Improper solicitation on company property without permission 5. Negligence in the performance of duties 6. Willful destruction or theft of company property 7. Violation of the company's policies or safety rules 8. Poor attendance 9. Physical or sexual harassment 10. Failure to maintain proper insurance and a satisfactory driving record (if you are required to drive on company business) 11. Other grounds as deemed A violation of the basic standards of conduct will result in disciplinary action. Serious violations may result in immediate termination.
Honesty and Ethical Behavior *(5/18/2015)*	As an employee of Your Company Name Here, you are expected to perform your job and conduct company business in an honest and ethical manner. The following are examples of dishonest behavior which will not be tolerated: • Willful falsification or misrepresentation on applications for employment or other work records; • Lying about sick or personal leave; • Falsification or alteration of company records or documents; • Falsification of expense reports, including attachment of false receipts; • Violations of non-disclosure, confidentiality, or proprietary information protection agreements; • Falsification or alteration of time reporting or attendance documents, including punching another employee's time card or causing someone to alter one's own records; • Willful misrepresentation of business terms to close a sale; • Willful or "convenient" misreporting and/or posting of results; • Alteration of a contract after the customer has signed the contract; • Unauthorized use, possession, or removal of company property, equipment, or documents.

| **Harassment** (5/18/2015) | As an employee of Your Company Name Here, you are expected to adhere to a standard of conduct that is respectful of all persons. Your Company Name Here will not tolerate any form of sexual harassment, such as unsolicited and unwelcome sexual advances, requests for sexual favors, or other verbal, physical or visual conduct of a sexual nature. (See Appendix, "Sexual Harassment is Forbidden by Law.") The company considers sexual harassment to be a major offense. Allegations will be investigated and, if substantiated, corrective disciplinary action will be taken, up to and including termination.

If you witness an incident of harassment, you have a responsibility to report it to your supervisor and/or the Administrator. If you believe you have been sexually harassed, you must immediately report the incident to your supervisor and/or the Administrator. If a non-employee harasses you during company time or on company premises, you and any employee witnessing the incident have the responsibility to report the incident to your supervisor. Your Company Name Here will take those steps within its power to investigate the complaint. |
|---|---|
| **Dress Policy** (5/18/2015) | Our company's image is often viewed in terms of your appearance and therefore you are expected to maintain the highest standards of personal cleanliness and present a neat, professional appearance at all times. Should you be improperly attired, the supervisor may send you home to change. If you fail to comply, you will be subject to disciplinary action up to and including termination. |
| **Confidentiality** (5/18/2015) | Protecting our company's information is the responsibility of every employee. Careless handling of information can seriously damage your reputation and that of the company: you are responsible to our clients/residents and co-workers to treat all information with the strictest confidence.

Due to the serious nature of a breach of confidentiality, failure to adhere to this policy will lead to immediate disciplinary action, up to and including termination. Company information must not be discussed with anyone outside of Your Company Name Here, and only with our employees with a "need to know." If such individuals request information, the question should be referred to the Administrator.

There may be situations in which people will question you in an attempt to gain such information. Should any such incidents arise, you should immediately report it and any other breach of confidentiality to your supervisor or to the Administrator. You are not permitted to make or remove copies of any Your Company Name Here records, reports, or documents without prior approval of supervisors. |

Conflict of Interest

(5/18/2015)

Your Company Name Here recognizes and respects your right to engage in activities outside of your employment, but reserves the right to determine whether such activities create a conflict with the company's interests. You are obligated to notify your immediate supervisor and the Administrator of a potential conflict of interest. Your Company Name Here may take whatever action it deems necessary, up to and including termination.

While it is impossible to list every circumstance that may create possible conflicts of interest, the following should serve as a guide to the types of activities which could create a conflict of interest:

1. A financial interest in an outside concern that does business with, or is a competitor of, the company (except where such ownership consists of securities of a publicly owned corporation regularly traded on the public stock market);

2. Rendering of directive, managerial, or consultative services to any outside concern that does business with or is a competitor of Your Company Name Here (including other care facilities), except with the company's knowledge and consent;

3. Acceptance of gifts of more than token value, loans, excessive entertainment or other substantial favors from fellow employees or any outside concern that does or is seeking to do business with Your Company Name Here, or is a competitor of, Your Company Name Here;

4. Representation of Your Company Name Here in any transaction in which a personal interest exists;

5. Unauthorized disclosure or use of confidential company information;

6. Outside employment, directly or through an intermediary, which can adversely affect your productivity or availability.

Performance Appraisal

(5/18/2015)

Your performance will be formally reviewed by your immediate supervisor upon completion of four months employment, and will be reviewed a minimum of once a year thereafter.

The performance appraisal is conducted to allow management to communicate to you how you have performed in relation to Your Company Name Here performance standards, and to discuss the objectives of the company and your objectives. The review should provide a basis for better understanding between you and your supervisor, with respect to your job performance, potential and development within the company.

Promotion From Within *(5/18/2015)*	Your Company Name Here believes that career advancement is rewarding for both you and the company. Whenever possible, Your Company Name Here will promote employees to new or vacated positions when job qualifications match job requirements. In addition, your supervisor is available to discuss transfer opportunities with you. Announcements of job openings will be posted in-house. If you are interested in applying for one of these positions, you should notify your supervisor. The Administrator will confirm to each candidate that he/she is being considered for a promotion or transfer.
Counseling and Discipline *(5/18/2015)*	The objective of counseling and discipline is to improve your performance. Certain performance deficiencies or offenses may result in immediate termination. Four types of disciplinary action may be used for counseling and discipline: oral counseling, written warning, suspension, and termination. Generally, these categories are successive; however, any step may be taken in any order as Your Company Name Here deems appropriate. The steps in the company's disciplinary procedure include, but are not limited to, the following: 1. At the first indication of the performance problem or violation of policy, your supervisor will meet with you to discuss the matter. You will be informed of the nature of the problem and the action necessary to correct it. 2. Should you continue to perform at a less than satisfactory level, or if policy or rule violations re-occur, the supervisor will issue a written warning to you. 3. In the event that you fail to correct performance problems or other situations that were described in previous formal written disciplinary notices, the supervisor will issue a final written warning to you. In some cases a work suspension may be necessary. 4. If you do not correct the problem, you will receive the final termination notification. There will be exceptions to using this disciplinary procedure in cases where good business practice demands immediate suspension or dismissal.

Benefits

Company Savings Plan

(5/18/2015)

You may elect to defer a portion of your salary in a 401-K plan. Your Company Name Here will make a 50% contribution, up to a maximum of 4% of your salary per year. You select the amount and investment type of your deferral. Your contributions to the 401-K plan will be made by payroll deduction. Complete details are available in the main office.

Eligibility:
All full-time and part-time employees working at least 1,000 hours per year are eligible for the 401-K plan. You are eligible for participation in Vision's 401-K plan upon completion of one year of employment, and upon reaching age 21.

Hardship Withdrawals:
By IRS regulation, withdrawals from the account may be made only if there is immediate and heavy financial need that necessitates the withdrawal. See plan details for eligible hardships.

Loans:
Your Company Name Here allows you to borrow up to 50% of your vested account balance as a loan. Vested balance must be a minimum of $5,000; loans may take six to eight weeks to process.

Payment at Termination:
You may choose either to "roll over" funds in your 401-K plan, or take an early distribution. See plan details for tax implications.

Vesting:
All of your contributions are immediately vested. Your Company Name Here contributions begin vesting after three "vesting computation periods" (see plan details for more information). However, if you terminate employment before the company contributions are vested, you forfeit any company contributions made to that date.

Medical Insurance

(5/18/2015)

If you are a full-time employee, you may participate in the company medical insurance plan (single or dependent contract) after completing four months of employment, and during open enrollment periods. Your Company Name Here will pay 50% of the cost of coverage for you and 50% of any additional family coverage; you are responsible for the balance through payroll deductions. If you are enrolled in the Section 125 Cafeteria Plan, your medical expenses may be applied to your flexible spending account. If you decline medical insurance, you will not receive payment in lieu of coverage.

Health coverage includes medical, vision, and prescription drug benefits. Complete terms of the coverage of the group insurance benefit plan are contained in the master group policy issued by the insurer, which is retained by the Administrator in the main office. Complete details on eligibility, benefits, filing claims and other important information are contained in the booklet provided to you at the time of your hire.

Section 125 Cafeteria Plan
(5/18/2015)

Your Company Name Here provides regular, full-time employees the opportunity to participate in a flexible benefits plan, the Section 125 Cafeteria Plan. Through pre-tax payroll deductions, you can create flexible spending accounts to pay for eligible healthcare and dependent care expenses not covered by other benefit plans.

Group medical insurance premiums (as applicable) will automatically be deducted and processed through the Section 125 Cafeteria Plan on a pre-tax basis unless the employee signs a Waiver of Benefits form. Complete details of the 125 Cafeteria Plan are available in the main office.

Dental Insurance
(5/18/2015)

If you are a full-time employee, you may participate in the company dental insurance plan after completing four months of employment, and during open enrollment periods. You may enroll in either a single or a dependent contract. Vision will pay 50% of the cost of coverage for you and 50% of any additional family coverage; you are responsible for the balance through payroll deductions. If you are enrolled in the Section 125 Cafeteria Plan, your dental expenses may be applied to your flexible spending account. If you decline dental insurance, no payment will be made to you in lieu of the coverage.

Pre-authorization of the dental carrier is required for all dental work in excess of $300. Complete terms of the coverage of the dental insurance benefit plan are contained in the master group policy issued by the insurer, which is retained by the Administrator in the main office.

Government Required Insurance
(5/18/2015)

Your Company Name Here will provide you with Workers' Compensation as required by state and federal law. You will pay a shared cost for other government-mandated insurance such as Social Security and Unemployment, and the full cost of State Disability through payroll deductions.

Vacation
(5/18/2015)

You are eligible to take vacation after one year of continuous employment. Vacation accrues from date of hire and is based upon net credited service. (See Employment section.) Temporary and part-time employees do not accrue vacation. Vacation does not accrue during any leave of absence.

During the first year with Your Company Name Here, the vacation accrual rate is 1.54 hours per pay period, up to a maximum of 5 calendar days per year. During the second through fourth years, the accrual rate is 3.08 hours per pay period, up to a maximum of 10 calendar days per year. The vacation accrual rate during the fifth year and beyond is 4.62 hours per pay period, up to a maximum of 15 calendar days per year.

Vacation (cont.)	The following guidelines apply to vacations: ***Holidays*** If a company observed holiday occurs during a scheduled vacation, you will be granted an additional day of vacation. ***Scheduling Vacation*** Vacation days should be taken within a year of being earned. If extra-ordinary circumstances prevent you from doing so, your supervisor may approve a maximum of one week of vacation for carryover into the next year. Any earned vacation not eligible to be carried over into the next year must be taken during the current year. If you fail to schedule your vacation, your supervisor will assign vacation time for you. You must complete a Time Off Request Form by March 15 of each year for the period between April and the following March. Scheduling preference for vacation time is based upon seniority of service and job level. Requests made after March 15 will be considered on a first-come basis. If you wish to cancel an approved vacation, your supervisor should be notified no later than one week prior to the scheduled vacation. ***Pay in Lieu of Vacation*** Vacation pay will not be granted in lieu of vacation time, except at termination. ***Payment At Termination*** You will be paid in a lump sum for all earned but unused vacation during the current year through the date of termination.

Holidays
 	
(5/18/2015)
	Your Company Name Here will provide paid holidays for all eligible employees. Part-time employees will receive pro-rated holiday pay. Payment will be made on the first pay period following your anniversary date.
	
	There are six paid holidays per year as follows:
	    New Year's Day
	    Memorial Day
	    Fourth of July
	    Labor Day
	    Thanksgiving Day
	    Christmas Day
	
	(Need to modify! caregivers likely must work some holidays!)

Holidays (cont.)	If one of the above holidays fall on Saturday, it will normally be observed on the preceding Friday. If one of the above holidays falls on Sunday, it will normally be observed on the following Monday.
	You must work your scheduled workday immediately before and after the holiday in order to be paid for the holiday, unless you are absent with prior permission from your supervisor.
Leaves of Absence *(5/18/2015)*	A leave of absence is defined as a specified period of time for approved time off, and may be granted under certain circumstances such as disability, family care, medical, jury duty, military service, travel/hardship, and personal reasons. The business needs of the company and the needs of the clients must be considered before a leave is approved. Leaves of absence are normally granted after earned vacation has been exhausted. Requests for a leave of absence must be made through your immediate supervisor. The following guidelines apply:

1. In general, you must have completed at least one year of continuous, full-time service to be considered for a leave of absence.

2. The company may change the approved start and end dates of a leave at any time, as business needs require.

3. Failure to return to work on an agreed date may be interpreted as your resignation.

4. Your Company Name Here will make an attempt to place you, upon return from a leave of absence, in the same position, or a similar position. However, such re-positioning cannot be guaranteed, except as required by law.

5. The length of a leave will be determined individually, in consideration of your needs and those of the company. Except where otherwise directed by law (e.g., pregnancy disability leave combined with Family Care and Medical Leave), the maximum leave of absence is four months.

6. On leaves of absence, company benefits (including contributions to the 401-K plan) cease to accrue. You will be allowed to continue your contribution to the company 401-K plan during a leave of absence.

7. During any Family Care and Medical Leave, your entitlement to healthcare benefits will continue up to twelve weeks on the same terms as if you continued to be actively employed. You are responsible for timely payment of 100% of your healthcare premiums. (See Appendix, "Family Care and Medical Leave Policy.")

Leaves of Absence (cont.)	8. Except in cases of travel/hardship leave, if you accept any other employment or go into business for yourself while on leave, it will be considered that you have voluntarily resigned your position with Your Company Name Here.

Sick Benefit *(5/18/2015)*	Upon the first anniversary of hire, full-time, hourly employees are given 24 hours (three days) of sick benefit; another 24 hours (three days) is given upon each succeeding anniversary date. Sick benefit is available only for your actual illness or injury, or that of someone in your immediate family, and must be taken in increments of two hours. You may be required to provide Your Company Name Here with a doctor's confirmation of your illness, and a doctor's confirmation that you are able to return to work. Unused sick benefits accumulate from year to year, up to a maximum of two hundred and forty (240) hours of sick benefit. After the maximum of two hundred and forty (240) hours is reached, no new sick benefit is given until the accumulated balance is reduced. If you are unable to report to work due to personal or dependent illness or injury, you must contact your supervisor immediately, and prior to your normal starting time. If you become sick during the day, notify your supervisor before you leave the work site. Failure to do so may result in disciplinary action. If you are hospitalized or out sick for more than seven (7) calendar days for an illness or injury that is not work-related, you must apply for State Disability Insurance (SDI) benefits. These benefits will be deducted from sick pay. Also, a Notice of Disability Benefits Received must be sent to the main office. The company will adjust sick pay to coordinate the two combined benefits, such that the combined total benefit does not exceed your normal rate of pay. Sick time taken after notice of resignation must be accompanied by medical confirmation of illness to be eligible for payment. Sick benefits are not paid upon termination of employment for any reason, nor can sick benefits be applied as extra vacation.

Bereavement Absence *(5/18/2015)*	You may request up to three days of Bereavement Absence with pay for attending the funeral for a member of your immediate family. Requests should be made through your immediate supervisor. Bereavement pay is granted only during periods of regularly scheduled workdays. Payment will be made on the payroll following the Bereavement Absence.

Health and Safety

Safety and First Aid

(5/18/2015)

Your Company Name Here is committed to providing a safe and healthful working environment for all employees, and expects employees to follow safe practices (including driving automobiles on company business). Each employee should make every effort to ensure that Your Company Name Here is a safe and pleasant place to work. If you are hurt or become ill, contact your supervisor or the Administrator for assistance. Your failure to report an injury may jeopardize your right to collect Workers' Compensation payments or health benefits.

The following safety guidelines must be followed:

1. All necessary measures will be taken to assure compliance with federal, state and/or local safety and health standards and regulations.
2. Safety programs will be offered to promote your safe work practices.
3. You must report all injuries, no matter how slight, to your supervisor.
4. Failure to adhere to these rules will be considered serious infractions of safety rules and will result in disciplinary action.

First aid kits and fire extinguishers are clearly marked and available in all Vision facilities. The following is a partial list of safety rules:

- Avoid overloading electrical outlets with too many appliances or machines.
- When using flammable items, such as cleaning fluids, exercise caution.
- Walk -- don't run.
- Use stairs one at a time.
- Report to your supervisor if you or a co-worker become ill or are injured.
- Ask for assistance when lifting heavy objects or moving heavy furniture.
- Smoke only outside of the Your Company Name Here buildings.
- Keep cabinet doors and file and desk drawers closed when not in use.
- Never empty an ashtray into a wastebasket or open receptacle.
- Sit firmly and squarely in chairs that roll or tilt.
- Wear or use appropriate safety equipment as required in your work. Avoid "horseplay" or practical jokes.
- Keep your work area clean and orderly, and the aisles clear.
- Stack materials only to safe heights.
- Always keep the safety of your fellow employees in mind.

Good Housekeeping *(5/18/2015)*	Good work habits and a neat and clean place to work are essential for job safety and efficiency. You should not eat at your workstation during company hours as this presents an unprofessional appearance and a potential hazard. At the end of the workday, files should be replaced and a general "clean-up" of all work areas should be accomplished before you leave. Materials should be kept in good working order at all times. Report any equipment that needs repair or replacement to your supervisor.
No Smoking Policy *(5/18/2015)*	To comply with the company's health and safety requirements, smoking is not permitted in any company offices or buildings; smoking is only permitted outside company buildings during your own time. If you are found smoking inside Your Company Name Here buildings you will be subject to disciplinary action. If you see others in violation of this policy, you must report infractions to your supervisor.
Alcohol/Drug Abuse *(5/18/2015)*	You are expected to be in suitable mental and physical condition while at work. Use of any mood or performance altering substances may negatively impact the safety and security of the company and its employees, and will therefore not be tolerated. If you possess, sell or use alcohol and/or illegal substances at the workplace, or come to work under the influence of such substances or under the unacceptable influence of prescription drugs, you are in violation of safe work practices and will be subject to disciplinary action, up to and including termination. Use of any substance, legal or illegal, that impedes your work performance and/or safety will subject you to disciplinary action, up to and including termination. If you report to work in a mental or physical condition which the company deems unacceptable, you may be asked to take a leave of absence for that day, or voluntarily submit to a drug test (prescribed and paid for by the company), or both.

Alcohol/Drug Abuse (cont.)	Your Company Name Here will analyze test results to determine whether your drug or alcohol usage poses a serious safety or health risk to you, other employees, or Your Company Name Here clients/residents. Being under the influence of drugs or alcohol during work hours will be presumed by Your Company Name Here to pose a serious safety and health risk. Any employee who has failed voluntary drug screening tests on two occasions will be terminated from employment. If you believe that you have a problem with substance abuse and need assistance, contact your supervisor for information about medical assistance and company insurance coverage.
AIDS Policy *(5/18/2015)*	Employees with AIDS or who are HIV-positive are not required to disclose this information unless job requirements and safety considerations for themselves, co-workers, and clients/residents make disclosure necessary. As with all personnel records, all forms and records will be treated with confidentiality. Employees with AIDS or who are HIV-positive will continue to receive all benefits to which they may be entitled. Your Company Name Here will not allow employees with AIDS or who are HIV-positive to be harassed, threatened, or intimidated, directly or indirectly, by any other employee. If you threaten or harass another employee, or violate the confidentiality provisions, you will be subject to immediate disciplinary action, up to and including termination. If you refuse to work with a person with AIDS or who is HIV-positive, you will be subject to immediate disciplinary action, up to and including termination.
Threats and Violence *(5/18/2015)*	Your Company Name Here strives to maintain a work environment free from intimidation, threats, or violent acts and behaviors, including but not limited to physical abuse, vandalism, arson, sabotage, use of weapons, carrying weapons of any kind on company property (including the company parking area), or any other act deemed by management to be inappropriate. You are responsible for reporting any such incident to your supervisor, and, if you believe there is a threat of safety to yourself or others, to the proper law enforcement authorities. The company reserves the right to search employees or their property without notice. Any employee who engages in threatening or violent behavior, including jokes or offensive comments related to threats or violence, is subject to disciplinary action up to and including termination.

Other Policies

Open Door Policy

(5/18/2015)

Your Company Name Here encourages all of its employees to freely discuss any job-related problem or incident, and will give careful consideration to each of these in a continuing effort to improve operations.

The goals of the open door procedure are to provide you with a means of being recognized and heard, and to alert management to sources of employee concerns. Your job will not be adversely affected in any way because you choose to use this procedure.

If you believe you have a problem, you should follow these steps:

1. First contact your immediate supervisor; be prepared to suggest solutions to the problem. Whenever possible, the supervisor closest to the problem will resolve problems or complaints.

2. If you are not satisfied with your supervisor's response, you may request an appointment to discuss the problem with the next level of supervision. Whenever possible, a response will be given within one week, and a written report forwarded to the Administrator.

3. If you are not satisfied, you should notify the main office in writing within one week. The Administrator and the Facility Lead will investigate and give you a written response within two weeks whenever possible.

4. If you are still unsatisfied, you may discuss the issue with the Administrator. The decision of the Administrator will be binding on all parties.

Regardless of the issues or problems involved, you must never abandon your job responsibilities (for example, by leaving the work site) without the approval of your supervisor.

Employee Communications

(5/18/2015)

We encourage you to bring your questions, suggestions and complaints to our attention. Careful consideration will be given to each of these in our continuing effort to improve operations; your job will not be adversely affected.

The following processes will assist continuing communication between management and employees.

Open Forum: CALLED SOMETHING ELSE?
In addition to on-going operational meetings, open communication forums for the expression of concerns and discussion of issues are held during working hours at least once each calendar quarter. All employees and supervisors in the department are required to attend the open forums.

Employee Communica-tions (cont.)	*Employee Newsletters:* APPLICABLE? Newsletters will be published biweekly to update employees on all pertinent company information such as competitive activity updates, new hires, policy changes, functions, etc. You are encouraged to submit notices and articles to the newsletter. *Bulletin Boards:* Information of interest and importance to you is regularly posted on bulletin boards at all company locations. We suggest that you look at company bulletin boards regularly. Information about safety, EEO policy, job opportunities, recreational events and social activities, and changes in the company will be posted.
Employee Suggestions *(5/18/2015)*	Your Company Name Here believes that its employees are an excellent source of suggestions for improvement of company operations, and you are encouraged to present your ideas for consideration. You may submit suggestions for the improvement of operations or procedures to the Personnel Manager on an Employee Suggestion Form. Suggestions must be written, organized, and detailed enough to show how implementation would save money, time, or material. Possible areas for improvements include: service, production methods, equipment, communications, safety, cost savings, or waste reduction. APPLICABLE? Your suggestion, if endorsed, will be forwarded to Department Heads for review. If a suggestion is approved and implemented, the employee who devised the suggestion or plan will receive a reward.
Personnel Records *(5/18/2015)*	The company maintains files of current and former employees consistent with its own needs and in order to comply with legal requirements. Only you and members of management with a legitimate need for such information have access to your files. Your personnel records are considered confidential and the company will ensure your right to inspect your personnel files. If you would like to review your personnel files, make a written request to your immediate supervisor. Files will be reviewed in the main office or other area designated by the Administrator. You may request and receive a copy of any documents containing your signature. However, you may not alter, add or remove records at the time of your review. If you wish to correct, copy, purge or amend information in the personnel file, you must first submit a written request and receive authorization from the Administrator.

Personnel Records (cont.)	Records available for your review include the following: 1. Test scores 2. Employment Applications 3. Interview Analysis 4. Salary Recap 5. Change of Status Forms 6. Performance Appraisal Forms 7. Counseling Review Forms 8. Other historical data that is directly related to your performance and qualifications 9. Personal medical information Records exempt from disclosure requirements are: 1. Those relating to the investigation of a possible criminal offense 2. Group insurance information 3. Career planning documents related to future or speculative action to be taken
Employee References *(5/18/2015)*	The company respects each employee's right to individual privacy, and will guard personnel information carefully. For this reason, only the Administrator is authorized to release information concerning current or former employees. If you are asked for information about a current or former employee, refer the request to the main office.
Documentation *(5/18/2015)*	All Your Company Name Here business transactions, including internal personnel matters, must be accurately and completely documented. Documentation must be factual and detailed, with the time, date, and location noted. Examples of business to be documented include customer service calls, accounts receivable, production, dealings with vendors and advertisers, and counseling and review sessions. When you prepare documentation, sign and forward the original copy to the appropriate Department Head.
Recycling and Conservation *(5/18/2015)*	Your Company Name Here recognizes its civic responsibility in preserving the environment. The Your Company Name Here recycling plan will benefit our environment, the company, and its workers. You are responsible for using supplies, equipment and utilities wisely. When recycling is feasible, two containers (one for white paper and one for computer paper) will be placed near each workstation, and near computers, printers and fax machines.

Recycling and Conservation (cont.)	All "contaminants" including colored paper, magazines, glossy paper, carbon paper, newspapers, soda cans, food, etc., should be kept out of the paper recycling containers. Covers, colored paper, plastic bindings, etc. must be removed before recycling the paper.
	Soda cans, soda bottles, and glass jars and bottles should also be recycled into designated recycling containers located in the lunch room, or other designated area.
	Supplies and equipment should be re-used until they genuinely need replacement. You are expected to practice energy conservation by turning off lights, equipment, and faucets when not in use.
Seminars, Conferences and Training *(5/18/2015)*	Your Company Name Here believes in continuing training for its staff, and from time to time may arrange for both formal and informal training programs. Attendance at company-sponsored educational seminars and conferences is mandatory.
	Attendance at additional educational seminars and conferences is encouraged, but must be carefully evaluated in order to ensure that such programs offer effective and appropriate training for both you and the company.
	If you would like to attend an outside event, submit a written request to your immediate supervisor. Supporting documentation on the program, such as literature, brochures, etc., should accompany the request. Seminars or conferences that require travel outside the local area and/or overnight accommodations require special approval from the Administrator.
	The criteria for approval for attendance at seminars, conferences, and other events include the following:

1. The seminar is necessary for your development in improving performance on the job.

2. Past attendance at seminars has favorably reflected on your job performance.

3. The event is necessary for public relations or marketing of the company.

In order to determine the value of each seminar, conference, or event as a potential development tool for other employees, feedback from every employee attending an outside seminar is required on the Event Critique Form, and forwarded to the Administrator.

Participation in Professional, Service and Industry Groups APPLICABLE? *(5/18/2015)*	Your Company Name Here supports your involvement in certain professional associations, industry groups and civic organizations, and may allow time off work and/or provide financial support of associated certain expenses. If you would like Your Company Name Here support in the form of contributions of cash or time off for outside organizations, prior written approval from your immediate supervisor must be obtained.
Advertising, Promotion, and the Vision Care Logo APPLICABLE? *(5/18/2015)*	Your Company Name Here wishes to present a standardized company image to its customers. ***Company Logo:*** Use of the company logo is restricted to pre-printed materials. You may not create additional material using the company logo without the approval of the Marketing Department, who will provide any artwork. ***Stationery:*** Only stationery authorized by the Administrator may be used. Company letterhead must not be used for correspondence between Vision facilities or offices. ***Business cards:*** Business cards may be ordered for you if your position responsibilities require you to represent the company with outside services, agencies, vendors, customers, etc. Your immediate supervisor must initiate requests for business cards or other Your Company Name Here stationery.
Correspondence *(5/18/2015)*	Your work, including all written correspondence, contributes to the image of Your Company Name Here; it is essential that your correspondence be factual, grammatically correct, and professional in appearance.

Security

(5/18/2015)

Your Company Name Here is committed to a safe and secure environment, and will prosecute all violations to the security of the assets of both its employees and the company, including proprietary company information. You are responsible for maintaining the security of company property, and for reporting any theft or other violation of security to your immediate supervisor. Non-exempt employees must be accompanied by a supervisor when on company premises after normal working hours.

The following guidelines are intended to illustrate security measures; additional procedures may be warranted in specific circumstances.

1. One employee will be designated at each location to maintain necessary petty cash; the amount of cash will be minimal, and must be locked at all times.

2. All employees should know the location of all alarms and fire extinguishers, and be familiar with the proper procedure for using them, should the need arise.

3. Keep file storage areas containing sensitive information locked.

4. Whenever possible and appropriate, secure computer hardware and software with lock devices.

5. Non-exempt (hourly) employees are not allowed on company premises after hours for any reason except with their supervisor.

6. Personal valuables must be properly secured at all times.

7. Employees must immediately report any suspicious activity to their immediate supervisor.

Use of Company Communications Systems

(5/18/2015)

The Your Company Name Here communication systems (intra-company mail, E-mail, telephone, voice mail) are to be used for company business only. The E-mail system is not private, and you must exercise caution when communicating proprietary information. All company communications should be made only to authorized employees with a "need to know."

The company has the right to monitor all communications to ensure that the systems are being used for company purposes only, to ensure that company policies on harassment are being followed, and to access your E-mail and/or voice mail when you are not available.

Use of Personal Auto on Company Business APPLICABLE? *(5/18/2015)*	Your Company Name Here sales employees are required to provide their own automobile transportation for business purposes, and to maintain their automobile in a safe, neat and clean condition. Sales employees are furthermore required to maintain in force an auto liability policy with $100,000 aggregate minimum coverage ($50,000 per individual/ $100,000 per occasion), to notify the Company of any policy changes, and to provide proof of coverage when requested. The company reserves the right to verify mileage with the odometer of the car when mileage vouchers are submitted for reimbursement. Your Company Name Here may periodically check Department of Motor Vehicles driving records. Any sales employee who is considered by the DMV to be a "negligent operator," or who loses his/her driver's license, may be terminated.
Employee Solicitations *(5/18/2015)*	Your Company Name Here does not allow solicitation that disrupts business, or subjects employees to pressure to unwillingly give support or make purchases. Any form of solicitation of employees by outside solicitors is prohibited. Employees may not solicit during working time for any purpose without company authorization.

Appendix

SEXUAL HARASSMENT IS FORBIDDEN BY LAW [1]

Employer Obligations	Sexual harassment in employment violates the provisions of the Fair Employment and Housing Act, specifically Government Code Sections 12940(a),(h), and (l).
	• Employers must take all reasonable steps to prevent discrimination and harassment from occurring.
	• Employers must act to ensure a workplace free from sexual harassment by posting in the workplace a poster made available by the Department of Fair Employment and Housing.
	• Employers must act to ensure a workplace free from sexual harassment by distributing to employees an information sheet on sexual harassment. An employer may either distribute this brochure (DFEH-185) or develop an equivalent document, which must meet the requirements of Government Code Section 12950(b).
Definition of Sexual Harassment	The Fair Employment and Housing Commission regulations define sexual harassment as unwanted sexual advances, or visual, verbal or physical conduct of a sexual nature. This definition includes many forms of offensive behavior and includes gender-based harassment of a person of the same sex as the harasser; the following is a partial list:
	• Unwanted sexual advances.
	• Offering employment benefits in exchange for sexual favors.
	• Making or threatening reprisals after a negative response to sexual advances.
	• Visual conduct: leering, making sexual gestures, displaying of sexually suggestive objects or pictures, cartoons or posters.
	• Verbal conduct: making or using derogatory comments, epithets, slurs, and jokes.
	• Verbal abuse of a sexual nature, graphic verbal commentaries about an individual's body, sexually degrading words used to describe an individual, suggestive or obscene letters, notes, or invitations.
	• Physical conduct: touching, assault, impeding or blocking movements.

---

[1] *This section, "Sexual Harassment is Forbidden by Law," is reprinted from the Department of Employment and Fair Housing brochure DFEH-185 (12/92)*

Employer Liability	All employers are covered by the harassment section of the Fair Employment and Housing Act. If harassment occurs, an employer may be liable even if management was not aware of the harassment. An employer might avoid liability if the harasser is a rank and file employee and if there was a program to prevent harassment. The harasser, as well as any management representative who knew about the harassment and condoned or ratified it, can be held personally liable for damages. Additionally, Government Code Section 12940(I) requires an entity to take "all reasonable steps to prevent harassment from occurring." If an employer has failed to take such preventive measures, that employer can be held liable for the harassment. An act of harassment, by itself, is an unlawful act. A victim may be entitled to damages even though no employment opportunity has been denied and there is no actual loss of pay or benefits.
Typical Sexual Harassment Cases	The three most common types of sexual harassment complaints filed with the Department are: • An employee is fired or denied a job or an employment benefit because he/she refused to grant sexual favors or because he/she complained about harassment. (Retaliation for complaining about harassment is illegal, even if it cannot be demonstrated that the harassment actually occurred.) • An employee quits because he/she can no longer tolerate an offensive work environment. (Referred to as a "constructive discharge" harassment case.) If it is proven that a reasonable person, under like conditions, would resign to escape the harassment, the employer may be held responsible for the resignation as if the employee had been discharged. • An employee is exposed to an offensive work environment. Exposure to various kinds of behavior to unwanted sexual advances alone may constitute harassment.

How the Law is Enforced	Employees or job applicants who believe that they have been sexually harassed may, within one year of the harassment, file a complaint of discrimination with the California Department of Fair Employment and Housing. The Department serves as a neutral fact-finder and attempts to help the parties voluntarily resolve disputes. If the Department finds evidence of sexual harassment and settlement efforts fail, the Department may file a formal accusation against the employer and the harasser. The accusation will lead to either a public hearing before the Fair Employment and Housing Commission or a lawsuit filed on the complainant's behalf by the Department. If the Commission finds that Harassment occurred, it can order remedies, including up to $50,000 in fines or damages for emotional distress from each employer or harasser charged. In addition, the Commission may order hiring or reinstatement, back pay, promotion, and changes in the policies or practices of the involved employer. A court may order unlimited damages.
Preventing Sexual Harassment	A program to eliminate sexual harassment from the workplace is not only required by law, but it is the most practical way to avoid or limit damages if harassment should occur despite preventive efforts.
Complaint Procedure	An employer should take immediate and appropriate action when he/she knows, or should have known, that sexual harassment has occurred. An employer must take effective action to stop any further harassment and to ameliorate any effects of the harassment. To those ends, the employer's policy should include provisions to: • Fully inform complainant of his/her rights and any obligations to secure those rights. • Fully and effectively investigate. It must be immediate, thorough, objective and complete. All those with information on the matter should be interviewed. A determination must be made and the results communicated to the complainant, to the alleged harasser, and, as appropriate, to all others directly concerned. • If proven, there must be prompt and effective remedial action. First, appropriate action must be taken against the harasser and communicated to the complainant. Second, steps must be taken to prevent any further harassment. Third, appropriate action must be taken to remedy the complainant's loss, if any.

Training of all Individuals in the Workplace

All employees must receive from their employers a copy of this pamphlet (DFEH-185) or an equivalent document. Any person may duplicate this brochure in any amount.

All employees should be made aware of the seriousness of the violations of the sexual harassment policy. Supervisory personnel should be educated about their specific responsibilities. Rank and file employees should be cautioned against using peer pressure to discourage harassment victims from using the internal grievance procedure.

For more information

**State of California
Department of Fair Employment and Housing**

For more information, contact your nearest
Fair Employment and Housing office:

Bakersfield
1001 Tower Way, #250
Bakersfield, CA 93309-1586
(805) 395-2728

Fresno
1900 Mariposa Mall, Suite 130
Fresno, CA 93721-2504
(559) 334-5373

Los Angeles
322 West First Street, #2126
Los Angeles, CA 90012-3112
(213) 897-1997

Oakland
1330 Broadway, #1326
Oakland, CA 94612-2512
(510) 286-4095

Sacramento
2000 "O" Street, #120
Sacramento, CA 95814-5212
(916) 445-9918

San Bernardino
1845 S. Business Center Dr., #127
San Bernardino, CA 92408-3426
(909) 383-44711

San Diego
110 West "C" Street, #1702
San Diego, CA 92010-3901
(619) 237-7405

San Francisco
30 Van Ness Avenue, Suite 3000
San Francisco, CA 94102-6073
(415) 557-2005

San Jose
111 North Market Street, #810
San Jose, CA 95113-1102
(408) 277-1264

Santa Ana
28 Civic Center Plaza, #538
Santa Ana, CA 92701-4010
(714) 558-4159

Ventura
5720 Ralston Street, #302
Ventura, CA 93003-6081
(805) 654-4513

TDD Numbers
Los Angeles   (213) 897-2840
Sacramento   (916) 324-1678

FAMILY CARE AND MEDICAL LEAVE POLICY

It is the policy of Your Company Name Here to allow qualified employees to take family care and medical leave as provided under the federal Family and Medical Leave Act of 1993 (FMLA) and the California Family Rights Act (FRA). Any absence by a qualified employee, which is taken for a FMLA and/or FRA qualifying purpose, will be counted against the employee's FMLA and/or FRA entitlement.

Qualified Employees

In order to qualify for family care and medical leave, an employee must have been employed for a year and must have completed a minimum of 1,250 hours of service during the previous twelve (12) months.

Allowable Leave Time

A qualified employee is entitled to take a maximum of twelve (12) weeks of family care and medical leave in a twelve (12) month period, measured backwards from the date any such leave commences.

Allowable Reasons for Family Leave

An employee may request family care and medical leave for any of the following reasons:

1. To care for a child after birth, adoption or placement of a child in the employee's home. Leave must begin within twelve (12) months after the birth, adoption or placement of the child.

2. To care for a spouse, child or parent with a serious medical condition. The employee must provide certification from a qualified healthcare provider documenting the need for the employee to provide such care.

3. For the employee's own serious medical condition if the employee is unable to perform the functions of his/her job. The employee must provide certification from a qualified healthcare provider stating that the performance of the employee's regular job duties would interfere with the employee's health. If the employee is requesting leave due to the employee's own pregnancy, childbirth, or related medical condition, the employee may be entitled to a maximum of four (4) months of California pregnancy disability leave.

Prior Notice	An employee should give thirty (30) days notice, if possible, of the need for family care and medical leave. If the employee is unable to give such prior notice, the employee should give notice of the need for leave as soon as possible after the employee learns of the need for leave.
Intermittent Leave	If the employee needs to take family care and medical leave on an intermittent basis to provide care for a child, spouse or parent with a serious medical condition or due to the employee's own serious medical condition, the employee may be allowed to take leave in intervals of not less than two hours. It may be necessary to temporarily transfer an employee to an alternative position for which the employee is qualified in order to accommodate recurring intermittent leave.
Use of Accrued Paid Time Off	An employee will be required to utilize any accrued vacation and/or other accrued paid time off at the beginning of any period of family care and medical leave. In addition, accrued sick leave must be utilized at the beginning of any leave requested due to an employee's own serious medical condition. All such paid time off utilized as part of a family care and medical leave will be considered part of an employee's entitlement to leave under the FMLA and FRA. After an employee's entitlement to accrued paid time off is exhausted, the remainder of any family care and medical leave will be unpaid.
Healthcare Benefits During Leave	During any family care and medical leave, an employee's entitlement to healthcare benefits will continue on the same terms as if the employee continued to be actively employed. An employee will continue to be responsible for timely payment of any employee share of the healthcare premiums. Failure of an employee to make such payments as required may result in the loss of healthcare benefits during a period of family care and medical leave. An employee will remain liable for any unpaid employee share of the healthcare premiums, which the employer is required to pay. Under certain circumstances, an employee may also be liable for the employer share of healthcare premiums if the employee fails to return from family care and medical leave.

Seniority and Job Position upon Return from Leave	An employee is entitled to be restored to the same or an equivalent position upon timely return from family care and medical leave, provided that all conditions have been satisfied. An employee who has taken family care and medical leave due to the employee's own serious medical condition will be required to provide medical certification that the employee is fit to return to work. Under specific and limited circumstances, an employer can deny reinstatement to certain "key" employees. An employee will not lose any seniority or the right to any accrued employment benefit as a result of taking family care and medical leave.
Additional Information	Additional information concerning an employee's entitlement to family care and medical leave is available from the Personnel Department. Information concerning employee rights under the FMLA and FRA is also available.

Community Care Facilities

Receipt of Employee Handbook

I have this day received a copy of the Your Company Name Here employee handbook, and I understand that I am responsible for reading the personnel policies and practices, including the appendix which contains the information entitled "Sexual Harassment is Forbidden by Law" and "Family Care and Medical Leave Policy," described within it.

I agree to abide by the policies and procedures contained therein. I agree to abide by the confidentiality policy, and will maintain all company information with the strictest confidence.

I understand that either the company or I may terminate my employment at any time, for any reason, with or without cause and without prior notice. The at-will relationship between Your Company Name Here and its employees may not be changed or affected in any way except by a written agreement which states that it is intended as a modification of a particular employee's at-will status, and is signed by _____ on behalf of Your Company Name Here.

If I have questions regarding the content or interpretation of this handbook, I will bring them to the attention of the Administrator.

_____
Employee Name (Please Print)

                                                    Date

_____   _____
Employee Signature

THIS COPY TO REMAIN IN EMPLOYEE HANDBOOK FOR EMPLOYEE INFORMATION.

Revised: 5/118/2015

Community Care Facilities

Receipt of Employee Handbook

I have this day received all pages of the Your Company Name Here employee handbook. I understand that I am responsible for reading the personnel policies and practices, including the appendix, which contains the information entitled "Sexual Harassment is Forbidden by Law" and "Family Care and Medical Leave Policy," described within it.

I agree to abide by the policies and procedures contained therein. I agree to abide by the confidentiality policy, and will maintain all company information with the strictest confidence.

I understand that either the company or I may terminate my employment at any time, for any reason, with or without cause and without prior notice. The at-will relationship between Your Company Name Here and its employees may not be changed or affected in any way except by a written agreement which states that it is intended as a modification of a particular employee's at-will status, and is signed by _____ on behalf of Your Company Name Here.

If I have questions regarding the content or interpretation of this handbook, I will bring them to the attention of the Administrator.

_____
Employee Name (Please Print)

                                        Date
_____   _____
Employee Signature

RETURN THIS FORM TO THE MAIN OFFICE

Revised: 5/18/2015

Made in the USA
Las Vegas, NV
19 September 2023

77826359R00031